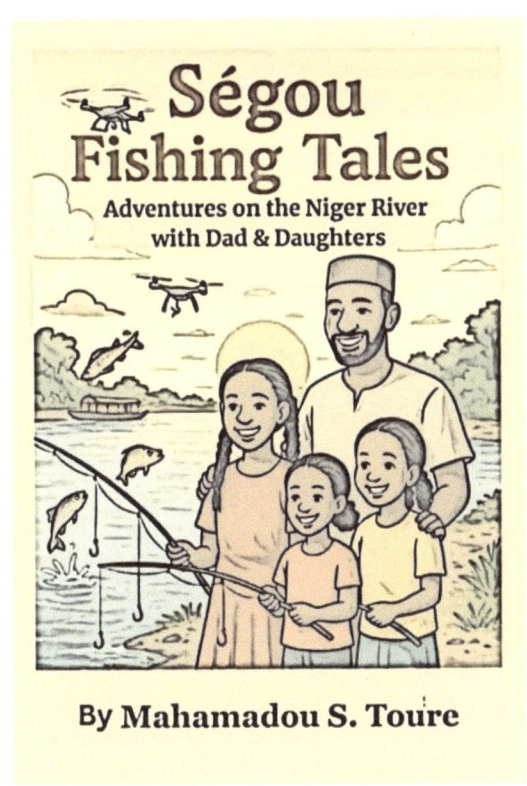

BabouConnect Publishing

Copyright © 2025 by [Mahamadou S. Toure]
All rights reserved.

No part of this book may be reproduced, stored in a retrieval system, or transmitted in any form or by any means — electronic, mechanical, photocopying, recording, or otherwise — without prior written permission from the author, except in the case of brief quotations used in reviews or articles.

Published by: **BabouConnect Publishing**

ISBN: 979-8-9939072-5-3 (Hardcover)

For permissions, contact:
sabilfalah@gmail.com

Disclaimer:
This book is based on personal memories and storytelling traditions. While inspired by real experiences, some characters and events are adapted for creative and educational purposes. **First Edition – 2025**

Dedication:

To my children — *may you always find joy by the river, laughter in the chaos, and memories in the **smallest fish**.*

Contents

Intro vii
Chapter 1 1
Chapter 2 3
Chapter 3 5
Chapter 4 7

Bonus Section
• *Fishing with Baba* 9
Author's Journey 13
Family Journal 15

— Introduction —
A River Full of Stories

My dear daughters,

When I was your age, the Niger River was my playground, my classroom, and my storyteller. Every ripple on the water carried secrets, and many fish had a different personality. The river taught me patience, courage, and laughter – sometimes all on the same day.

Fishing in Ségou wasn't just about catching fish. It was about family, friendship, and fun. We didn't always bring home the biggest catch, but we always came back with the best stories.

I want you to know these stories, not just because they're **funny** but because they're ours. This river runs through our history, our memories, and our hearts. One day, I want you to stand by its banks, cast your line – maybe even fly a drone above it – and feel the same excitement I felt when I was young.

So today. I'll tell you the secrets of four special fish:
The dogfish, the fearless jumper.
The nana, the sunset dancer.
The dodo, the mischievous bait thief.
And the lightning fish, the little shock of the river.

Lesson of the Dogfish

"When life jumps at you...
don't panic. Step back,
stay calm, and keep pulling."

Chapter One—
The Dogfish: The Fearless Jumper

**Ah, the Dogfish...
the river's little fighter.**

This one is no joke, my daughters — if you catch a dogfish, everyone on the riverbank will know.

The dogfish is long and slim, like a small snake, maybe 20 to 50 centimeters. It has sharp little teeth like a baby shark and a red tail that flashes when the sunlight hits it. Beautiful to look at... but don't let that fool you. This fish is wild.

Back then, we didn't have fancy fishing poles or drones. We used a simple silver lure — shiny, like a little diamond — and threw our lines about 20 or 25 meters out into the river. Then we waited, hearts racing, holding our breath.

"... no mistakenly hit.".

Here's the funny part; when you hook a dogfish, sometimes you feel the line go loose and think, "Ah, I lost it..." But no! This little monster has a trick — it doesn't run away, it runs toward you!

I remember the first time its secret When you catch a dogfish, you don't stand still. You step back, slowly, carefully, maybe even 20 meters away from the riverbank.

its

Lesson of the Nana

"Life has its seasons. Some days are quiet, but if you wait patiently, your moment will come — and when it does, take it with both hands."

SÉGOU FISHING TALES

Chapter Two — The Nana: The Sunset Dancers

Ah, my daughters, if there's one moment on the Niger River you must never miss, it's when the sun touches the horizon and the nana arrive.

The nana are small, bright-green fish with golden lines glimmering along their sides, their bellies shining gold as they dance beneath the fading light.

And then, when the time came, someone would take a handful of cereal or watermelon and toss it into the water. Suddenly, you'd see the river come alive. First, a few ripples. Then, the surface explodes with movement — hundreds, sometimes a thousand nana, all swimming together, flashing green and gold, rushing to feed.
Everyone shouts, laughs, and moves fast — because this is your chance. Even if you spent the whole day catching nothing, this is the moment the river gives back.

I remember standing there one evening, line in hand, watching the shadows shift beneath me. Suddenly, the water below turned silver-green with the flashes of nana. I cast my line once — pulled in one. Cast again — another! My friends and I laughed so hard, shouting to each other over the chaos:
"Nana bɛ na! Nana bɛ na!" ("The nana are coming! The nana are coming!")

"Nana bē na! Nana bē na! ("

Lesson of the Dodo

"In life, not everything goes your way—sometimes you lose your bait. But if you can laugh about it, you've already won."

😄 Chapter Three — The Dodo:
The Mischief Maker

Ah, my daughters... if there's one fish in the Niger River that will make you laugh until your stomach hurts, it's the dodo. Small, stubborn, and always causing trouble — this little guy is the river's prankster.
The dodo isn't big, maybe the size of your hand, but don't be fooled — it has sharp little teeth and can steal your bait faster than you can blink! We used to warn each other about its hiding spots under rocks and cracks near the riverbank. But if you forget... oh, that's when the fun begins.
I remember one day, five of us were fishing together. The first friend lost his bait. Then the second. By the third, someone shouted:
"Ahhh! Dodo again!"
We laughed so hard we couldn't breathe!
And here's the funniest part — when you actually catch one, the dodo inflates its belly like a little balloon, making a "bloop-bloop" sound, as if it's saying:
"Let me go! I didn't mean it!"
Most of the time, we'd release it back into the river, letting it swim away to cause trouble for the next fisherman.

So, my daughters, when we go fishing one day, I'll teach you a trick:
- Avoid throwing your line where the dodo hides... unless
- You want to see the funniest little fish in Ségou puff itself up and complain!

Because that's the magic of fishing in Ségou — it's not just about the fish you catch, but the memories you create together.

Lesson of the Lightning Fish

"Life will surprise you when you least expect it. Sometimes the shock knocks you back, but if you can laugh and keep fishing, you've truly won."

Chapter Four
The Lightning Fish: The Hidden Thunder

Ah, my daughters... now we come to the fish that makes even the bravest fisherman jump, scream, and run out of the water like a goat being chased!   This little one is rare — you might fish for months and never see it. But when you do... you'll never forget it.

It's small, about hand-sized, hiding quietly under rocks along the riverbanks. They wait patiently, still as stones, until something tasty floats by. At first, you won't feel a thing. But as the line gets closer, a soft vibration travels up through your rod. Then — the moment you disturb their hiding place — the lightning fish reacts in a flash. It was unexpectedly caught and — ZZZZ-AP! A shock shot up my arm, through my legs, into my feet. My whole body jumped before I even understood what was happening!
Without thinking, I dropped the line and ran out of the water faster than I've ever run in my life. We all burst into laughter so hard our bellies ached.

' One of my friends shouted through his laughter: Ahh, it's just a fish! Keep yourself together and cast again!'
 We couldn't stop laughing — the river, the chaos, and the surprise made that moment unforgettable.

Ségou Fishing Tales

BONUS SECTION
Fishing With Baba

"Because fishing is not just about the fish you catch…
it's about what you learn along the way."

1. Baba's Top Fishing Secrets

- **Dogfish Trick** — Use a shiny silver lure to attract dogfish
- **Nana Ritual** — Toss a handful of watermelon into the water near where you stand by sunset.
- **Dodo Defense** : Avoid rocky spots unless you're ready for some laughs— Dodo is mischievous
- **Lightning Fish** Warning —Avoid touching a wet fishing line during a lightning storm — safety first!

2. How to Fish With a Drone

- Use water shoes—always remember, keep hands
- Stay together as a family near the water

3. Baba's Safety Rules

- Wear water shoes
- Keep hands dry when handling the line
- Stay together as a family near the water

Our Family Fishing Journal

Date: _____

Location: _____

Who Came With Us: _____

What We Caught: _____

Some of Baba's favorite sayings we'll never forget:

Baba's Fishing Sayings

- "If the line is too quiet, the dodo is nearby!"
- "No watermelon, no nana!"
- "Don't fish with anger — the river will feel it."
- "Catch a dogfish? That's dinner tonight!"

Author's Journey

It all began on an ordinary day, with a *drone fishing* commercial flickering on TV. Then came the curious voices of my children: "Daddy, what kind of fish is that?"

That simple question unlocked a river of memories—the sounds of laughter, splashing waters, and endless childhood tales along the banks of the Niger River. One story led to another, and before I knew it, I was sharing the fishing adventures of my youth: the patient waits, the unexpected surprises, and the lessons nature taught us along the way.

From those little conversations, a bigger journey began. What started as a passing moment became a way to preserve memories, connect generations, and celebrate the timeless stories hidden in everyday life.

Family Journal

Fill the next few pages with writing, drawing, and treasuring your best fishing memories!

Made with Love in Ségou

Made with Love in Sëgou

Made with Love in Ségou

My Favorite Fishing Moment

Made with Love in Ségou

www.ingramcontent.com/pod-product-compliance
Lightning Source LLC
Chambersburg PA
CBHW041135130526
44582CB00031B/129